Make Your Own
Cake TOPPERS

For my lovely Mum and Dad

Make Your Own
Cake TOPPERS

Darren
Allford

WHITE OWL

AN IMPRINT OF PEN & SWORD BOOKS LTD.
YORKSHIRE – PHILADELPHIA

First published in Great Britain in 2022 by
Pen & Sword WHITE OWL
An imprint of
Pen & Sword Books Ltd
Yorkshire – Philadelphia

ISBN 9781526774545

A CIP catalogue record for this book is
available from the British Library.

Printed and bound in the UK, by Short Run Press Limited, Exeter.

Design: Paul Wilkinson

Pen & Sword Books Limited incorporates the imprints of Atlas, Archaeology,
Aviation, Discovery, Family History, Fiction, History, Maritime, Military, Military
Classics, Politics, Select, Transport, True Crime, Air World, Frontline Publishing,
Leo Cooper, Remember When, Seaforth Publishing, The Praetorian Press,
Wharncliffe Local History, Wharncliffe Transport, Wharncliffe True Crime and
White Owl.

For a complete list of Pen & Sword titles please contact:
PEN & SWORD BOOKS LIMITED
47 Church Street, Barnsley, South Yorkshire, S70 2AS, England
E-mail: enquiries@pen-and-sword.co.uk
Website: www.pen-and-sword.co.uk

Or
PEN AND SWORD BOOKS
1950 Lawrence Rd, Havertown, PA 19083, USA
E-mail: Uspen-and-sword@casematepublishers.com
Website: www.penandswordbooks.com

Contents

Introduction

WELCOME! The fact that you have opened this book can mean only one thing. You need to create, right? Whether this is because you need that extra-special cake topper for that extra-special cake or because you have a sudden urge, a need to go off on a creative whim – you need to create and you've come to the right place. Taking time out of our busy lives to make brilliant things, rather than just buying them, should be encouraged. You'll find that making magic happen with your hands is a simple pleasure that should be indulged. Whatever brought you here, your adventure is about to begin and I sincerely hope that it is one that you'll find incredibly rewarding.

If you were to do a quick online search you would find a heap of experts claiming that by simply tapping in to your own creative energy, you'll find evidence that suggests you're improving your overall health. Sound far-fetched? Try it. If you properly apply yourself to something and give it your full attention and concentration, you can't also spend that time worrying about the everyday stresses that we usually allow to buzz in the back of our minds. Now, if the thing we're properly applying ourselves to is also something that we enjoy doing? We might as well be meditating.

Everyone has some creativity in them that's bubbling to get out. All that stands between that creativity being released and the finished creation is knowledge. Armed with the knowledge and using the right tools and a whole heap of imagination, anybody can become a maker. The best way to approach making is never to see it as a chore. It should never be something that makes you release a heavy sigh or something that makes you roll your eyes. The secret is to see it as playing. Watch a child play for inspiration and you'll see how much energy children joyfully put into creating wondrous things, gleefully exhausting themselves purely out of an untarnished passion to indulge their own imagination. The moral of this story is 'don't grow up, it is a trap' and the plan in this book is to reconnect with that inner child, high-five it, roll up your sleeves and have some fun. You are absolutely up for the challenge and you'll be amazed at what can be created in the process.

So, cake toppers! A simple cake can be completely transformed into a show stopper if it is decorated with a bit of love. Not everybody is a home baker, but nearly all of us will have a celebration every now and then that requires a cake. A cake that in a crowded room would make one person squeal 'that's for me!' Once you know how, you'll see that you – yes you! – will be able to transform an inexpensive shop-bought sponge into something that's really extra special. If you're a home baker too then you definitely need to add this string to your bow so that you can transform your own freshly baked treats into the showstoppers they were destined to be.

In recent years and along with the rise of social media, cake trends have become increasingly popular and simple cake decorating has evolved into elaborate must-haves, especially with creative home bakers and crafters willing to go that extra mile. Wonderful as all these trends are – and they really are – a cake that has a bit of height to it, that has been placed on a covered board, that has been properly iced, tied with a ribbon and topped off with one of the little creations in this book is going to have just as much impact and will indeed cause a high-pitched squeal from the cake recipient.

The range of different toppers you can create is limitless; if you can think of it, you can almost always find a way to make it. In this book, we're going to learn how to make twelve different toppers that will teach you a whole range of skills and techniques. I firmly believe that making these cute little creations will arm you with the knowledge to head out on your own creative adventures and make things that you see in your imagination as well as in fabulous books like this!

Whilst creating the toppers in this book remember not to be confined to using exactly the colours and features that are suggested. If by coincidence the designs match your requirements exactly then by all means follow them to a T and you'll produce perfect replicas, but feel free to adapt the creations to make them unique to you and your needs. Always go with the gender of the cake recipient and their skin tone, hairstyle and colour, and fashion choices and personality. Always allow yourself to go off on a tangent and make your creations unique to you and the person you're making them for. Our mantra from this point on is 'there are no mistakes, just choices we haven't thought about yet.'!

Chapter 1 will give you all the information you need prior to starting out on your first topper. This chapter is where you'll learn about the differences between creating with fondant and creating with clay, the tools that will help make your creative life a little easier and lots of other tips to get you ready and raring to go. Please give this chapter a read first, this is the non-practical knowledge bit and will ease any creative insecurities you may have. After the first chapter, feel free to read the rest of the chapters in your own order. Some makes will initially appear more advanced or daunting than others, but it really is just about time. Some will take longer to create, but they are ALL within your reach. Remember that you're playing so enjoy allowing yourself that extra hour or so of playtime if you can spare it.

If you post any of your creations online, whether they are replicas of the designs in this book or fabulous creations of your own, it would be a real treat to see them. Include the hashtag #howtomakecaketoppers so that we can cheer you on from the side lines!

How exciting! Let's get started.

Darren

CHAPTER ONE

The Ingredients

AS MENTIONED IN the introduction, this chapter is the only one in this book that doesn't require you to roll up your sleeves. This is the theory bit where we'll go on a brief journey of discovery which will ease any anxieties you may have regarding your forthcoming creative adventure. Here we will talk through the materials you can use to make your creations and the tools that will make your creative life that little bit easier.

MATERIALS

The two most common materials used to create cake toppers are fondant or polymer clay and they are what we'll focus on using in this book. You can decide which material you choose to work with for each character; you'll quickly work out which works best for you. They are both really good fun to work with so let's look at them in a little more detail:

Fondant

The obvious benefit of creating with fondant is that the entire cake is edible. It's a cake so we already know the person you're making this for has a sweet tooth, and they won't be cross about getting to eat the topper too. Fondant is also a slightly easier material to work with as it is already soft and pliable, a quick roll in between warm palms and you're good to go. Working with fondant does take longer than it would with clay, purely because you need to let fondant toppers dry before they can reach the top of a cake. Admittedly not always, but more often than not you need to let lots of little components dry out before you can assemble the final piece. Fondant is much heavier than polymer clay too; it means that you'll need to avoid designs that are top heavy or they will topple over. The cost of fondant can vary; most supermarkets now stock it and the majority of it is of decent quality. You can get a better-quality fondant known as sugar paste or gum paste in most craft shops or online and this will give you a better finish, but supermarket brands are good enough as long as they are fresh. You should expect to pay between £2 and £3 for 250g and avoid cheaper options as poor quality fondant will tear and give you a rough finish. We wouldn't want that would we?

Polymer clay

The number one benefit of using polymer clay is that the recipient gets to keep their topper forever. A treasured keepsake: people will be just as excited to know they can keep their mini-me as they would be about eating it. This is an option that wedding couples often choose, or somebody who has asked for a topper of their best friend or family member, furry or otherwise. Clay is a great material to work with; it enables you to create designs that just are not possible with fondant. This is because when you bake your finished design it fuses all components together, which gives you a solid structure that supports itself – compared to a fondant structure that would need supporting. Your topper will also lose most of its weight after baking so you can create elaborate designs that stay intact and upright that you simply couldn't create with fondant, they would break as soon as you looked at them. You really need to put some thought into the architecture of the structure if your design is in fondant, whereas the clay appears to almost defy gravity. For these reasons you'll fall in love with it as a material to work with.

However, if fondant is an easy material to work with, clay is trickier. If cold, it becomes really tough and you'll need to get it back to room temperature before working with it otherwise you'll end up with many a bruised palm trying to warm it up. A tip if this happens is to put it on a heat-resistant tray on a radiator to soften it before you work with it. Even when soft it has a completely different feeling to fondant; it has a much tighter consistency. Clay is available in most good craft shops, but it can be expensive at between £2 and £3 for 50g. Shop around online, there are some really good deals out there for sets that contain a great selection of clay as well as tools and ideas. Clay won't thank you for trying to move it once you've started to create so make your clay toppers directly on to a piece of greaseproof paper. You can then lift it straight on to a baking tray before popping it into the oven. With that in mind, the first pieces you lay down will be visible on the reverse of your topper once baked so make sure you begin nice and tidy. All of the toppers in this book need to be baked at the lowest temperature on your oven for a maximum of twenty-five minutes. Smaller pieces will take slightly less. Times for each topper are given at the end of each chapter.

Cornflour

Dusting your work surface before starting out on a new creation is essential, for both fondant and clay, as both will stick to your surface without it. It's also good to use to smooth out edges and surfaces; just add a little flour to your finger beforehand. Icing sugar may seem the obvious choice, but you'll quickly realise that it actually has tiny little grains in it, especially noticeable with clay creations. Cornflour has a much finer grain.

Glue

You may need some of this on hand for the your more elaborate clay creations; anything that looks as though it might fall off at some point can be secured with a dab of glue to give you peace of mind. Always make sure you use non-toxic glue.

Water

Water is the glue for your fondant creations. Always keep an egg cup of water on hand when you're creating. Top tip; only half fill it as it will inevitably get knocked over at some point!

Lustre

Lustre is an edible, powdery substance that comes in all colours and lots of glittery variations. When mixed with water it becomes a paste that can be painted on to your fondant or clay creations. The gold version of this wondrous stuff is used in quite a few chapters in this book, it really does lend itself to a bit of grandeur quite beautifully. Gold is just the tip of the grandeur iceberg though, as lustre comes in every single colour you can possibly think of and with all kinds of effects from metallic to glittery to pearlised. Lustre costs around £5 for a small pot; however, you'll get a lot of out of one tiny pot so if you enjoy making the creations in this book and want to make more of your own, an investment of a few pots will really ramp up the fun.

Edible ink

Craft shops and online shops sell all sorts of pens that enable you to write and draw on your fondant designs, but sadly they don't lend themselves to drawing on the clay models, although you could always draw on the clay models with thin permanent markers after they have been baked if your creations require you to. People often use edible pens to add pupils in eyes or details on mouths or eyebrows. They have only been used once in this book, so are not an essential buy for these makes, however, you might enjoy using them if you wanted to experiment.

Tools

There are a few key tools that will make your life easier but, apart from the dowelling, none of these are absolutely essential and you can make these toppers without them. Howwever for £10 or under you can treat yourself to a lovely bunch of nice-to-haves which will make the making easier and the finish more professional and consistent. Let's have a talk through some of these.

Dowelling

You'll find what works for you quickly enough. If you're going to see the dowelling you might want to match it to the design – a pack of sturdy plastic straws should cover most bases for fondant designs. Obviously plastic won't work with polymer clay as it will melt in the oven so wooden BBQ skewers work well for both clay and fondant and might be considered the most environmentally friendly option. Unfortunately, paper or biodegradable options will get soggy in a cake – so always avoid those.

Modelling tools

Cake decorating is big business and if you search online stores you'll be inundated with all sorts of inventions that you'll be told that you have to have to make your creations with. The truth is that you don't need most of them, but a pack of basic modelling tools really would make your creative life so much easier and you can pick up a pack online or in some supermarkets for about £5. They are sold like a pack of eight pens but instead of ink nibs they have handy tools on each end, therefore, in total you'll have sixteen invaluable tools to play with. Each has a different job, some create patterns, some cut out shapes and some make indentations, but one or two you'll find yourself using over and over again. One used repeatedly in this book is the one that creates a perfect smiling mouth. It has a tiny semicircle on the end of it and this will give you either the happiest or saddest of mouths. We'll refer to this as the smiling tool in this book. The second one to look out for has a perfectly round ball on the end of it and you'll use this often when creating indentations for eyes. You get what you pay for with these so avoid the bargain offers – you don't want a crooked smile or uneven eyes!

Cutters

You can buy cutters for an enormous selection of shapes in craft and online shops. If you can think of it, you can probably buy a cutter for it. Generally speaking, most of these are not necessary, but if you have a hunt online you can find some really great packs of assorted cutters that might be a wise investment, especially as cutters seem to be the exception to the rule where budget verses quality is concerned. For as little as £5, you can get thirty cutters including circles, squares, hearts, leaves and all sorts of other treats. A great little investment as you'll use some of them over and over again, but as always, you can make anything using your hands so if that's your preference then please do create your shapes yourself.

Paintbrushes

Because the fondant designs are held together using water as glue it is great to have an array of different size brushes to work with. Again, not essential, as one small one will work fine, as will your finger.

Cocktail sticks

Humble cocktail sticks will become your new best friend – you'll use them to support different parts of most of the toppers in this book so you'll need a good stock of them. They are also really handy for making tiny indentations and turning fondant into fur, as you'll discover shortly!

Rolling pin

The rolling pin will become your constant companion whilst making toppers, but as a rule avoid wooden rolling pins as you'll quickly discover that they will leave grain marks in your designs. You can pick up inexpensive plastic rolling pins in budget shops or online, or glass works well too. You want a nice smooth finish so remember to keep lightly dusting your work surface as well as the rolling pin itself.

Health, Hygiene and Safety

Before you begin to make your fabulous creations, there are a couple of practices that I recommend you follow. They apply to everything you make so I'll add a little reminder in each chapter, just in case you need a prompt when you're so absorbed in what you're making!

Hygiene protocols

Hygiene first: always clean your surfaces properly before you begin making a new topper and remember to wash your hands thoroughly. Dust your surface with cornflour and keep some close by and dust as and when things start to feel a little sticky.

You'll also want to wash your hands and surfaces when changing between different colours. Your hands may look clean but you'll be amazed at how stained they can get from rolling different colours between your palms. Some people use latex gloves and change them for each colour but most people prefer to work without them – whilst remembering to wash their hands regularly.

Safety

A safety point that cannot be stressed enough is that, as you know, these edible creations have cocktail sticks hidden inside all of them. These are great for support but they are not great for eating and would be a nasty surprise, so please make sure that you always remember to dismantle and remove the sharp sticks before giving the sweet treat to somebody to nibble on.

So that's about all of the preparation and information we can squeeze in without rolling up our sleeves, friends! It is now time to dust that surface down, wash those hands and get ready to roll, quite literally. Don't forget to come back to Chapter 1 as and when you need to refresh yourself on anything.

Time to play! Good luck. You are going to be brilliant.

CHAPTER TWO

Girls' Night Out

ANYBODY SEEING A mini version of themselves perched on top of their birthday cake is bound to be delighted, so making tiny replicas or your friends and family looking fabulous whilst doing their favourite things will probably become your favourite toppers to make. In this chapter we're going to make a mini-me of that party animal that we all know and love, the birthday diva all dressed up and ready for a night on the town with her gal pals. For this particular birthday girl, we're going for the highest of camp. Think high heels, pink hearts, cha-cha dresses and possibly pompoms.

This topper is being made from polymer clay so that the birthday girl has a keepsake reminder of her fabulousness for years to come, but if you prefer you can use fondant to make her so that she gets to be eaten too. The only difference is that she'll need a good forty-eight hours to dry out compared with clay taking twenty minutes to bake, so it is whatever works best for you and your schedule.

Remember the hygiene protocols before you begin; make sure everything is clean and you have plenty of materials for cleaning down between colour changes.

Start by rolling out some soft pink clay and then cutting out a heart shape. If you don't have a cutter go freehand, you've got this! Your character and their birthday number will be on this heart so keep that in mind when deciding on the size. Place a piece of dowelling along the length of the heart leaving at least 7cm of it to go into the cake as shown in image 2.

Next it is time to cover the heart shape with whatever design you desire; the more

Image 2.

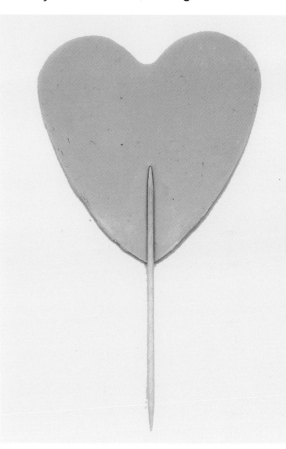

Image 3.

unique to the recipient the better. The design will not only look great but it will also secure the dowelling in place. If time is a factor, the simplest way to do this is to take a second piece of clay the same shape and size as your design and place it on top, thus sandwiching the dowelling between the two halves. The design in this chapter may take a little longer but is still very easy and MUCH more fabulous. First roll out some thin purple clay and cut out several purple discs with a circle cutter and roll lots of balls of fondant in different colours between your fingers as shown in image 3. Don't stress with measuring them, they don't all need to be exact.

Next, place the discs all over the heart, keeping them as close together as you can. Then take the smaller balls and place them in between the small gaps, pushing down gently with the round tool to secure them as shown in image 4 – and ta-daaa! – Your unique background is complete!

Roll out a long thin sausage of pink fondant and secure it by

Image 4.

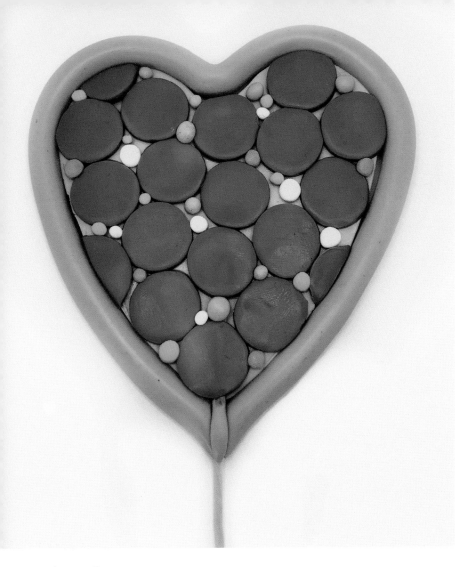

Image 5.

Image 6.

pressing it slightly to the outside of your design to make a frame as shown in image 5.

Now it is time to create your mini birthday girl. As with a few chapters in this book, this stage is easier if we roll out all the eight shapes in image 6 before we assemble. So as shown, roll out two arms, two legs, the top part of the body, the bottom part, the neck and the head. Adjust these if you've got a particular body shape you want to create.

Place the pieces on top of the design as shown in image 7. Secure them all by pressing down gently, but before doing that make sure to play about with the poses of your character – are they practicing yoga? Painting? Dancing? Jogging? Or like this gal, just striking her best pin-up pose!

For the face, take a generous pinch of clay that matches your character's skin tone and roll between your palms to make a smooth ball. Dust your palms with cornflour if they get too hot, to avoid the clay getting sticky. Using the tool with the ball on the end of it, gently push two indentations where you want the eyes to be and add two tiny black balls for pupils. Roll a tiny ball of skin tone for the

Image 7.

Image 8.

nose and add a mouth with the smiling tool. You'll find that mouths and eyebrows will suddenly change a character's expression so why not experiment with these before securing as shown in image 8.

Next the hair. Roll out two long thin sausages of fondant and carefully twist them together. Repeat this several times to give yourself plenty of material to work with as shown in image 9.

Then place two strips across her hairline to give her a base

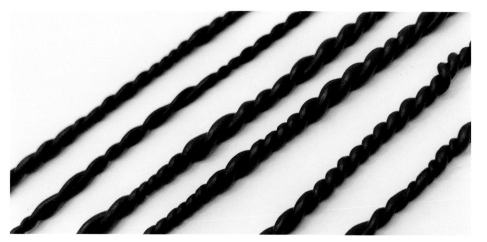

Image 9.

Image 10.

Image 11.

covering as shown in image 10.

Twist a strip around itself creating a small twisted ball, repeat and place them on top of her head as shown in image 11.

Next, place a twist coming from in between them, flicking to the left to give her a fringe as shown in image 12. Like she just left the salon, huh? Fabulous!

But as always, go as big or as small with the hair as you want. Your friend with the sleek bob COULD have an enormous beehive for the night! Add the number of the birthday by rolling out thin sausages and tracing out the numbers – much easier than you might think – and make sure that you go for a colour that won't get lost on your design.

Hands are much easier to create than you might first think. Roll out a

Image 12.

little egg shape in the colour of the skin tone of your character and gently push it flat, dusting some cornflour on the surface and on your finger first to avoid sticking. Then take a sharp knife and cut four little slits at one end, thus creating four fingers and a thumb! If you're very careful you can separate them to create movement and wrap them around objects your character wants to hold.

Stiletto shoes for a design like this are pleasingly simple to create yet extremely effective. Just take a foot-size piece of clay in skin tone and roll it into an egg shape. Cut out a flat disc in whatever colour you want the shoe to be and wrap it around one side of the egg, creating the shoe and the foot. Add a heel by rolling out the thinnest sausage to match the shoe colour. Add her hands and stilettos as shown in image 1 and she's ready for the oven! Naked, yes, as this design includes a material outfit that we're going to add after she has been baked.

As with all clay creations in this book, bake this one on the lowest heat setting on your oven.. Once it has reached temperature, place the topper on greaseproof paper on a baking tray and bake in the centre of the oven for twenty minutes, after which you should carefully remove from the oven and leave on a cool surface until completely cold.

Her outfit you could, of course, make from clay, lots of evenly cut little pink sausages with tiny balls on the end would look incredibly cute, but why would we deny her an actual fringe for her cha-cha dress? You can get fringed ribbon really cheaply online, and the cha-cha look it gives her will completely transform the creation. Cut small pieces of ribbon and secure with a dab of glue as shown in image 13.

Image 13.

Now all that's left is this famous night out that everybody has been talking about! And then wait for them to squeal. They always squeal. If you're feeling extra fabulous and you want to secure a string of pompoms around the outside, knock yourself out. But you know … it isn't compulsory. Flick back to image 1 for the finished piece. Fabulous stuff indeed.

CHAPTER THREE

Fun at the Farm

IF YOU WERE to ask a panel of mostly very small people what they love they would probably tell you that they mostly love cute things and they mostly love animals. Go ahead, ask a panel of mostly very small people. See? This means that, generally speaking, a cute farmyard cake will be a winner for the wee ones. In this chapter we're going to learn how to make a pig, a sheep and a rooster. Once you've mastered these, you'll have the confidence to attempt all the other friends that live on the farm. The horse, the cow, the goat – hours of fun! But actually, not 'hours' of fun because this is a really quick and easy make as it is mostly made out of lots of discs. A real crowd pleaser for very little effort. These designs are made from fondant but because of their simplicity they will only need a few hours to dry out. And the little people? They would rather eat them than have clay ones to keep.

Image 2.

Remember the hygiene protocols before you begin; make sure everything is clean and you have plenty of materials for cleaning down between colour changes.

To make the pig, take a generous pinch of pink fondant and roll between your palms to make a smooth ball. Dust your palms with cornflour if they get too hot, to avoid the fondant getting sticky. Roll out two pink balls and flatten into fat discs, make one about twice the size of the other. Push a cocktail stick through them to join together, securing with water as shown in image 2. Leave to dry in a cool, ventilated area for about an hour.

To make the rooster repeat these steps using orange discs. With a sharp knife, cut gently into the bottom half as shown in image 3, marking where the wings will be placed. Leave to dry in a cool, ventilated area for about an hour.

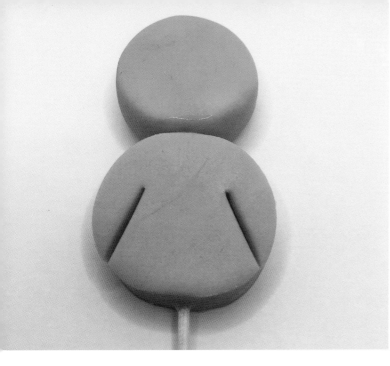

Image 3.

Image 4.

To make the sheep repeat the steps using white and brown discs, but this time push a cocktail stick into the white disc and lay the smaller brown disc on top, securing with water as shown in image 4. Again, leave to dry in a cool, ventilated area for about an hour.

For the sheep's face cut out two brown circles for the cheeks, a tiny black one for the nose and for the eyes, two white circles for the outer, two smaller black circles for the inner and two tiny ones for the pupils. Secure all these with water as shown in image 5.

Staying with the sheep, roll out twenty little white balls, varying slightly in size. Don't flatten these down into discs, you want these to remain nice and round. With a little water, secure them all over the white body, avoiding the brown face area as shown in image 6.

To finish off the sheep, add two slightly larger balls for feet and

Image 5.

Image 6.

pinch two small brown circles together slightly to make the ears. Secure all these pieces with water as shown in image 7.

Back to the rooster! To add the beak, start off with a small ball of yellow and shape it into a fat triangle, placing one edge to cover the bottom half of the face as shown in image 8. With a knife, press a line down the middle and with a cocktail stick add a dot either side of the line.

Image 8.

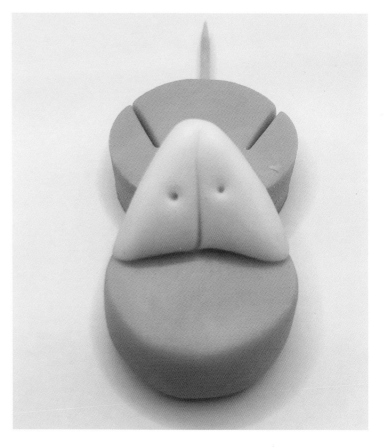

Add eyes by cutting out two white circles for the outer, two smaller black circles for the inner and two tiny ones for the pupils. To make the wings, cut out a thin circle the same size as the body. Cut this in half and add indentations with a cocktail stick to create feathers as shown in image 9.

Add the wings to the body, placing them on the lines

Image 9.

you made earlier with the knife as a guide, securing them with water. To finish him off, roll out four little tear shapes in red and place two under the beak and two on top of the head as shown in image 10.

Last but certainly not least our friend the pig! Add eyes as with the others, ears as you did with the sheep and a snout that's an oval disc with two holes poked with a cocktail stick. Add feet by cutting out small squares and indenting

Image 10.

trotters with a cocktail stick. Secure all the pieces with water as shown in image 11. Allow at least an hour for all pieces to dry in a warm dry space.

Then perch those cuties on top of a brightly iced cake and let the fun commence!

A word of warning: before you let anyone nibble on this sweet treat, remember to remove the cocktail sticks to prevent a nasty surprise!

CHAPTER FOUR

Oh Baby!

BABY SHOWERS AND gender reveal parties are more popular than ever and it has become 'a given' that these affairs will have all manner of sweet treats readily available for guests to enjoy. At the centre of these sugary feasts, you'll find the baby shower cake; perched on top of that is where you come in with the cute factor! The baby topper in this chapter is cute with a capital C, a much easier challenge than attempting some elaborate stork or a circus full of fun – and it still ticks the 'adorable!' box. This design is being made from fondant because when everybody squeals 'Oh it's so cute I could eat it!' you should probably let them. Ideally, this is one of the designs that you'll get to build directly on to the finished cake. If not, cut out a circle of fondant, let this dry completely and build your design on to this so that you can lift the finished character on to the cake. You can of course make it out of clay if you would rather, as it would, after all, make a really lovely keepsake.

Image 2.

Remember the hygiene protocols before you begin; make sure everything is clean and you have plenty of materials for cleaning down between colour changes.

Start by taking a generous lump of fondant that matches your character's skin tone and roll between your palms to make a smooth sausage. Dust your palms with cornflour if they get too hot, to avoid the fondant getting sticky. Stand the sausage upright, flattening the bottom slightly. Push a cocktail stick through the middle and add a small, flat disc on top as shown in image 2.

For the face, again take a generous pinch of fondant that matches your character's skin tone and roll between your palms to make a

Image 3.

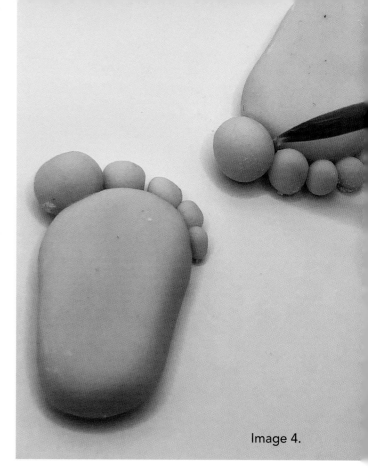

Image 4.

Image 5.

smooth ball. Roll out some white fondant and cut out two discs for the eyes, placing these on to the face and adding two tiny black balls for pupils and roll a tiny ball of skin tone for the nose. Finally, create a dummy by cutting out a small, thin disc and attaching a small, thin line curled into a semicircle as shown in image 3.

Next, make the feet by shaping small flat rectangles, rounding off the corners with a dry finger. Add the toes by rolling tiny balls, each slightly bigger than the last as shown in image 4.

Place the body on to the cake and secure the head with a dab of water as shown in image 5.

Now roll out as many little white balls (bubbles) as you want, but at least twenty, some slightly larger and some slightly smaller. Build these

from the bottom up to cover the baby, placing the feet at the front and securing everything with water as shown in image 6.

Make whatever bath toy you want to; in this chapter we've gone for a classic rubber duck, again very easy to create but incredibly cute too. Roll out two yellow balls, one smaller than the other. Pinch the end out of the larger ball to create the duck's tail, secure the smaller ball on top, add a small beak and poke eyes and feathers with a cocktail stick as shown in image 7.

Add some tiny bubbles on the baby's head and – ta-daaa! – A really easy make but one that will bring to life even the most basic of iced cakes.

Before you let anyone nibble on this sweet treat, remember to remove the cocktail sticks to prevent a nasty surprise!

CHAPTER FIVE

The Furry Family Member

PEOPLE LOVE, LOVE, love their pets and once people know you can make cake toppers it won't be too long before you're asked to create a furry family member – so it was essential to include a chapter on these beloved friends in this book. Just go ahead and tweak your design to reflect the recipient's pet – breed, colour, collar, favourite

Image 2.

toy, wonky ear – the more quirks the better! This design is being made from fondant and will need about twenty-four hours to dry out. If your schedule needs it sooner, do by all means make your characters out of clay.

Remember the hygiene protocols before you begin; make sure everything is clean and you have plenty of materials for cleaning down between colour changes.

Because this is a fairly easy make, start by making all the pieces prior to assembly as shown in image 2. Essentially you want to roll egg shapes and then just roll out the tops to create the different shapes – one body, four legs, one head and two ears.

Take the body and stand it upright, flattening out the bottom slightly, pushing a cocktail stick

Image 3.

Image 4.

Image 5.

through the middle as shown in image 3. Now take the back legs and wrap them around each side of the body, securing with a dab of water.

Next, stand the front legs upright against the front of the body, securing with a dab of water as shown in image 4.

Now it is time to make this friend furry! This trick is easy and so effective. Take a cocktail stick and dig it into the fondant and then pull it out again at an angle, teasing a little piece of fondant to stick out. As you continue to repeat this action you'll see the furry friend begin to appear. Add a circle of fondant to one of his paws to give him a little patch as shown in image 5.

For the head, add another patch on one eye and attach the

ears with water. Rest one ear on a paintbrush so that when the head is standing up, one of his ears will be slightly tilted forward as shown in image 6.

For the face, add two small black balls as eyes with two tiny white balls on top. The nose is another egg shape, then use the smiling tool for the mouth and pop a cute pink tongue inside as shown in image 7. Set everything aside to dry for twenty-four hours before popping the head on top of the body and securing with water. If your dog wears a collar, cut out a colourful flat disc and insert it in between the head and the body.

The cat is made in exactly

Image 8.

the same way – although make the cat's head more oval than egg shaped. To add stripes just lay thin strips of a different colour on top of your shape as shown in image 8.

Pick out the fondant in the same way across the two colours as shown in image 9. Add tiny triangle ears for the cat. And of course, don't forget the tail!

Image 9.

See image 10 for the fully assembled cat, complete with fish bones and collar. Don't forget to tag us into your furry creations online with #howtomakecaketoppers. We can't wait to see your family member mini-me's!

Before you let anyone nibble on this sweet treat, don't forget to remove the cocktail sticks to prevent a nasty surprise!

Image 10.

CHAPTER SIX

The Gamer

AS WE'VE ALREADY established in this book, seeing a mini version of themselves sitting on top of their birthday cake will always light up the recipient's face with a smile; even moody teenagers who can't tear themselves away from their computer games will crack one when they see themselves. This one is tried and tested, you have to look closely because it is only a very small smile, but it is there! Have a good think about what you can include to guarantee recognition. Favourite T-shirt or trainers? Hairstyle, colour, do they wear glasses or a baseball cap? As with all of the designs in this book you can tweak the style, ethnicity and gender to mirror your birthday star. This topper is being made from polymer clay so that the birthday boy can forever be reminded of how moody he once was as a teenager, but if you prefer you can use fondant to make it so that it gets to be eaten too. The only difference is that a fondant design of this size will need a good forty-eight hours to dry out versus clay taking twenty-five minutes to bake, so it is whatever works best for you and your schedule.

Remember the hygiene protocols before you begin; make sure everything is clean and you have plenty of materials for cleaning down between colour changes.

Image 2.

Let's start by creating the legs. Roll yourself out a long, thin sausage in blue, twice the length of the character's legs, bend in the middle and cut both ends off with a sharp knife. As always, dust your palms with cornflour if they get too hot, to avoid the clay getting sticky. Next, roll a small blue ball and flatten it into an oval disc. This is going to be the top of the trousers so again adapt the size to fit the trousers. Place the disc on top, pressing down gently to attach. Cut out tiny blue rectangles for belt loops, placing on either side of the disc as shown in image 2.

Next, add two more belt loops to the front

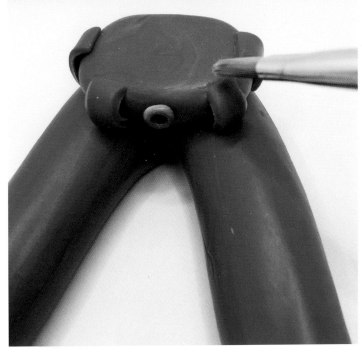

Image 3.

and a tiny ball of a different colour for a button which will instantly become one when you push it in place with a cocktail stick, as shown in image 3 – magic!

For the body, roll out a fat green stumpy sausage. Trim one end off with a sharp knife and smooth the other end to create shoulders, pushing a cocktail stick through the middle as shown in image 4. Push the body into the middle of the blue disc, securing the body to the legs. Go rogue with your T-shirt; you can make this as unique and exciting as your heart desires, but it is also the perfect place to put the birthday number. This one is very easy as you can see, just a thin red sausage and two flat circles creates the figure 18.

For the shoulders and sleeves of the T-shirt, roll out some red clay and cut out a circle the width of the body. Cut the circle in half, placing the two halves on each shoulder, pushing them gently in place as shown in image 5. Add a small red circle through the cocktail stick to create the T-shirt neck hole.

Image 4.

Image 5.

Image 6.

Now it is time for some funky sneakers! You could, of course, give your teenager bare feet or socks; however, although these shoes may look tricky to create it is actually just a matter of cutting out several different shapes in different colours and placing them altogether. In the process of making these you're going to have a 'wowsa!' moment when you realise just how easy this making lark really is. As with a few other makes in this book, let's make all of the pieces of the sneakers before we assemble, it is much easier that way. See image 6 and do not be daunted! All we're doing is playing and cutting out some cute little shapes! Start by rolling out some yellow clay and cut out two thin rectangles and a circle, cutting the circle in half. Next the soles of the shoes; roll out two little fat orange sausages and flatten them before pinching slightly in the middle to create the rounded sole shape. Next, roll out some pink clay and cut out two thin rectangles,

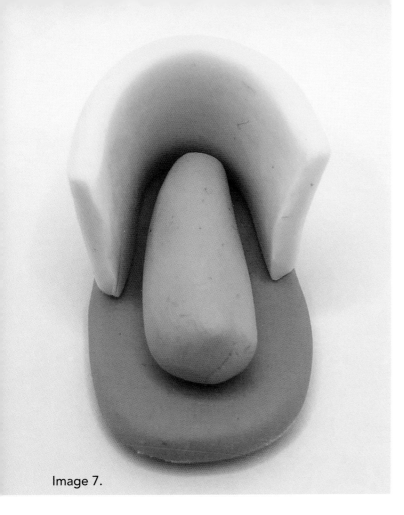

Image 7.

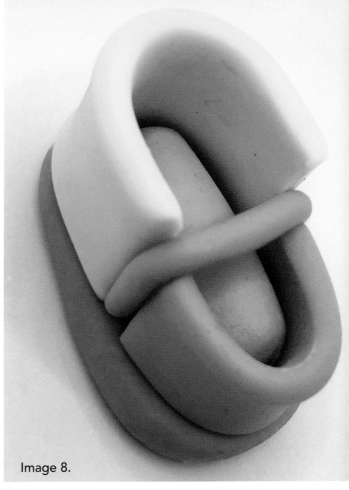

Image 8.

just slightly smaller than the yellow ones. Roll out two thin pink sausages, then cut out two red stars (or replace with little red circles if you don't have a star cutter). Lastly, roll out some thin blue clay and cut out two little rectangles. That's it! You are done!

Now to assemble them – which is a walk in the park after all that rolling, smoothing and cutting! Firstly, roll out two little fat sausages for the feet in whatever colour you want the socks to be – purple for this guy. Take the orange sole and place the purple foot on top of it, wrapping the flat yellow rectangle around the back as shown in image 7.

Next, take the pink rectangle and wrap it around the front of the foot. Then take the pink sausage and lay it across the foot, hiding the join between the yellow and pink rectangles as shown in image 8.

Now take the yellow semicircle and place it on top of the pink band at the front to create the sneaker toe. Then place the blue rectangle on top of the toe, creating the tongue as shown in image 9. Add some grooves with a sharp knife to mimic laces.

Next, make grooves with a sharp knife on the bottom of the sole before attaching the red star to the side of the sneaker as shown in image 10. Don't celebrate being done just yet, you still have to make the other one! Extra marks if you were brave and made them at the same time.

For the socks, simply roll out two little fat sausages in purple and

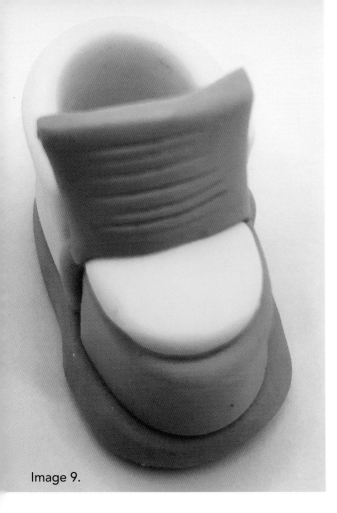

Image 9.

Image 10.

then a small ball of skin tone to the very top of it. Smooth the sides of the sausage, flattening at each end before scoring randomly with a sharp knife to create the rolls in the socks as shown in image 11.

Now you can attach the legs to the socks and the socks to the sneakers! Gently press them together as shown in image 12. There is no need to secure these with cocktail sticks, the oven will fuse them together.

Image 11.

Image 12.

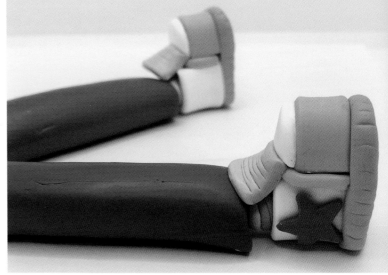

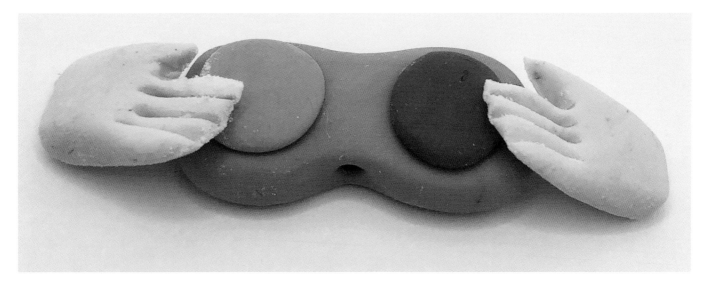

Image 13.

Next, we're going to make the very important controller for the very important computer console! Roll out a grey sausage and flatten it with your finger. Cut little triangles in the middle to create the controller shape and finish by placing a red and an orange ball of clay on top of each rounded end and secure in place by flattening them as shown in image 13. On top of the controller buttons, you need to place two little hands. Roll out two little egg shapes in skin tone and gently push them flat, dusting some cornflour on the surface and on your finger first to avoid sticking. Then take a sharp knife and cut four slits at one end, thus creating four fingers and a thumb! Carefully separate them to create movement and wrap them around the controller so that the hands are holding it.

Now it is time for the birthday boy's head. Take a generous pinch of clay in skin tone and roll between your palms to make a smooth ball. Dust your palms with cornflour if they get too hot, to avoid the clay/fondant getting sticky. Roll out some white fondant and cut out two discs for the eyes, placing these on to the face and adding two tiny black balls for pupils. Roll a tiny ball of skin tone for the nose and add another tiny ball for the mouth, poking in the middle with a cocktail stick to create that 'I couldn't take my eyes away from the screen if I wanted to' look as shown in image 14. As always, do play about with the mouth before deciding as it will totally change your character's expression.

To assemble, roll out two thin skin-toned sausages for the arms, cutting gently with a sharp knife to help them bend and thus create the elbows. Place the arms under the red T-shirt sleeves and press gently to secure. Then attach the two wrists to the two hands,

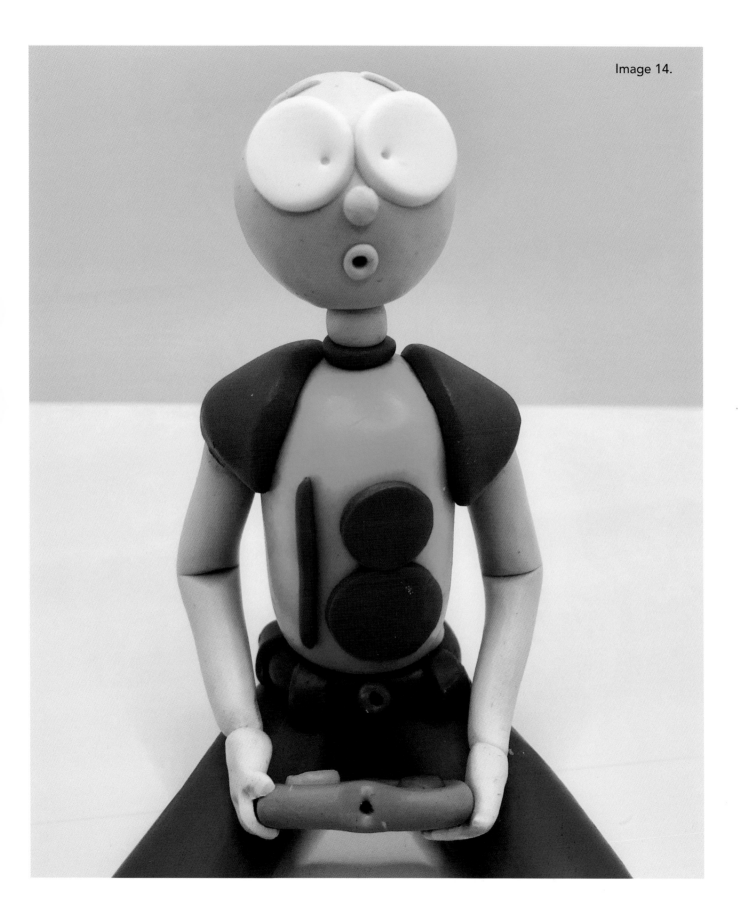

Image 15.

Image 16.

placing the controller between his legs. Add a thin skin-toned sausage for the neck and then push the head down on to the top of the exposed cocktail stick. Add surprised eyebrows on a slant in whatever colour you've chosen for your hair.

For the hair, let's roll out the pieces that we need before we assemble, see image 15. Start by rolling two small, thin sausages for either side of his head, a long, thin sausage to create a frankly magnificent quiff and then you need a thin piece of clay to cover the back and top of the head. Create this by rolling out a thin square, cutting off the top two corners and smoothing them off with your finger. Then score little grooves along the flat edge with a sharp knife, pulling the bottom two corners out a little bit to create a slight flick.

Now for the assembly. Take the large piece of hair and wrap it around the back of the head as shown in image 16.

Next, add the two thin sausages either side of the head as shown in image 17.

Now it is time to make the very important earphones that you'll rarely see a moody teenager without! These are very easy to make; roll out two little balls of black and push an indentation in to the middle of each one. Next, roll out some grey and cut out a long, thin strip as shown in image 18.

Place the grey strip across the head and then hide each end with one of the black balls, indented side showing as shown in image 19. Finish by adding that quiff we were talking about and voila! He's ready for the oven. As with all clay creations in this book, bake this one on the lowest heat setting on your oven. Once it has reached

Image 17.

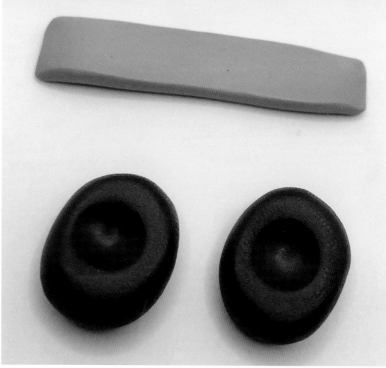

Image 18.

temperature, place the topper on greaseproof paper on a baking tray and bake in the centre of the oven for twenty-five minutes – after which you should carefully remove from the oven and leave on a cool surface until completely cold.

Finish by gluing a little piece of string from the controller to the console with a tiny dab of glue as shown in image 1. All that's left is for this chap to take his place on top of that teenage cake! Keep your eyes peeled for the aforementioned smile. Blink and you'll miss it.

Image 19.

CHAPTER SEVEN

Forest Fairy

FAIRY STORIES ARE not just for small children, they are also for the bigger ones who refused to grow up – and lots of us still enjoy losing ourselves in tales about elves, trolls, fairies, imps and gnomes and the adventures they have in the forest. Imagine how much fun you can have creating little outfits for these cuties from things you find in the woods? There is no high street in the forest (as far as we know).

In this chapter we're going to be making our topper out of polymer clay so that when the cake has been eaten, she can be popped into a plant pot or even live her best life in the garden under a toadstool. This design is for a forest fairy, but let your imagination run wild, especially with the hair and clothes. Have fun with it.

Remember the hygiene protocols before you begin; make sure everything is clean and you have plenty of materials for cleaning down between colour changes.

Image 2.

Let's start with the face. Take a generous pinch of clay that matches your character's skin tone and roll between your palms to make a smooth ball. Dust your palms with cornflour if they get too hot, to avoid the clay/fondant getting sticky. Roll out some white fondant and cut out two discs for the eyes and place them on to the face. Next, cut out one skin-toned colour disc the same size as the eyes, cut it in half and place on top of the white eyes to create sleepy eyelids as shown in image 2. Add two tiny black balls for pupils, thin black sausages for eyelashes and roll a tiny ball of skin tone for the nose. Add a mouth with a tool, give your character whatever expression you want – are they surprised? Curious? This one is happy because she loves her new hat. More on that later.

Image 3.

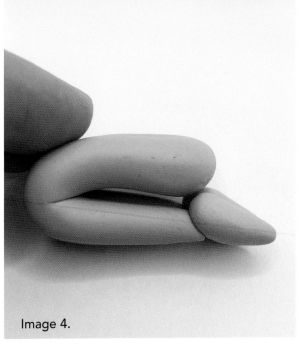

Image 4.

Image 5.

Next, roll out a long, thin sausage in your skin tone and bend in the middle, creating the legs, cutting a small indentation in the middle to create the back of the knees as shown in image 3.

Then bend the legs in on themselves to create the kneeling position and add small tear shapes as feet as shown in image 4.

To make the body, roll a small fat sausage in whatever colour your character wants to wear, and push a cocktail stick through the middle. Add a small, thin sausage for the neck, leaving the stick visible at both ends as shown in image 5. Play about with proportions, they don't always have to be realistic. This fairy has a very long neck and that might well be the key to her cuteness.

Cut out a small disc in the same colour as the body, place that on top of the kneeling legs and then push the cocktail stick with the body attached through both the disc and the legs as shown in image 6.

If you have a leaf cutter, cut yourself out four leaves and place them around the disc to create a skirt as shown in image 7. If you don't have a leaf cutter you can easily create your own by making little fat tears and flattening them and adding vein marks with a toothpick.

Cut out another two leaves to match the skirt and place these along the shoulders. Then cut out four more leaves in contrasting colours and place these around the skirt as shown in image 8. Next, cut out little flowers and dot them wherever you think some might have fallen and again, if you haven't got flower cutters go freestyle and let your creativity run wild.

Attach her head by pushing it on to the exposed cocktail stick as shown in image 9.

Image 6.

Image 7.

Image 8.

Image 9.

Image 10.

Image 11.

Now for the hair! Go all out. Characters who make their clothes out of leaves don't have boring haircuts. Clay will also support creations that would be incredibly fragile if they were made out of fondant so make the most of it and be creative. I'm starting by wrapping a very long, thin piece of clay around itself, starting in the middle, to create a complete covering of the head as shown in image 10. Next, roll out three small sausages and curl into small spirals, placing them either side and on top of the head.

Then roll out two thin sausages for the arms with little cuts to create the bend and place them underneath the leaves on the shoulders as shown in image 11. Next, roll out two slightly longer, fatter sausages and place them on top of her head, one in front of the other as shown in image 12. Lastly, add one long, thin curl to give her a fringe, flicking it up at the end.

Now she needs an apple as a hat. Roll a small green ball, squash it ever so slightly, roll a tiny sausage for a stalk and pop it into the middle and finish off with a tiny leaf as shown in image 13.

Now she needs some flowers – because she's a flower fairy, so adapt this to whatever your chosen character would have an armful of. Roll out five thin sausages for the stems, ideally a different colour from the outfit. Just add a little black or brown to your green fondant to make it darker, or yellow to make it lighter. Lay the stems on her lap and cover the tops with flower heads. Finish by adding little hands (which are much easier to create than you might first think). Roll out two little egg shapes in her skin tone and gently push them flat, dusting some cornflour on the surface and on your finger first to avoid sticking. Then take a sharp knife and cut four little slits at one end of each shape,

Image 12.

Image 13.

Image 14.

thus creating four fingers and a thumb. Carefully separate them to create movement and wrap them around the flower stems as shown in image 14.

And you're done! As with all clay creations in this book, bake this one on the lowest heat setting on your oven. Once it has reached temperature, place the topper on greaseproof paper on a baking tray and bake in the centre of the oven for twenty minutes, after which you should carefully remove from the oven and leave on a cool surface until completely cold.

Add wings by cutting out two simple heart shapes and brushing them with glitter. Bake these separately from the fairy and when everything has been baked and has cooled completely, attach them to her back with a little glue. The reason for not attaching the wings prior to baking is that they might well droop during the baking process. Now she's ready to be perched on top of her cake (before eventually realising her dream of sitting underneath a toadstool in the garden). Hoorah!

CHAPTER EIGHT

Everybody Loves a Unicorn

IN THIS CHAPTER, we're going to address one of the trends mentioned in the introduction and that's the fact that … well, that everybody loves a unicorn. Small and big people alike, there seems to be something completely enchanting about these mythical cuties and folk can't get enough of them, so let's supercharge the cute factor with this topper and see how loud we can get that 'Aaaaaaaaaw!'.

Don't forget the hygiene protocols before you begin; make sure everything is clean and you have plenty of materials for cleaning down between colour changes.

The best place to start is with the body. Take a generous lump of whatever colour fondant you want your unicorn to be; this beauty is going to be yellow. Roll the fondant between your palms to make a smooth ball. Dust your palms with cornflour if they get too hot, to avoid the clay/fondant getting sticky. Flatten the bottom only slightly so that the unicorn doesn't roll away. Then roll out some yellow fondant and cut out a small, flat disc, placing it on the top of the body to create a little fat neck as shown in image 2.

Next, make the face by rolling another yellow ball. Roll out some white fondant and cut out two discs for the eyes, placing these on to the face and adding two tiny black balls for pupils. Instead of a nose we're going to need a nice big snout. The easiest way to achieve this is to roll out a fat sausage and cut yourself off a nice chunky slice. Secure

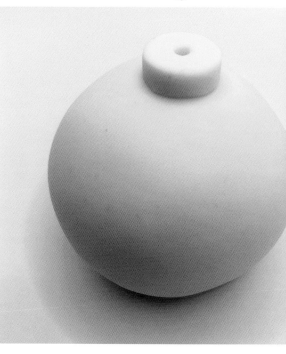

Image 2.

Image 3.

Image 4.

with water and add nostrils with a cocktail stick. Lastly, add a smiley mouth with the smiling tool as shown in image 3.

Next, add eyelashes by rolling the tiniest of sausages, and cheeks by flattening tiny pink balls, securing everything with water as shown in image 4.

The arms and legs can be made in the same way as the snout. Roll out a long, thin yellow sausage and cut off four slices. Roll two of them out slightly to make them thinner, and flatten four pink balls to attach to the bottom of the hands and feet as shown in image 5.

Image 5.

Anybody thinking that unicorns don't have noses or arms, a gentle reminder about the mythical bit, so it is ok.

Now it is assembly time! Attach the head, arms and legs to the body with cocktail sticks, securing them all with water as shown in image 6.

To create the horn, roll two thin sausages and twist them around each other like an ice cream swirl. Then roll between your fingers gently. If you feel like being extra special, you can paint the horn gold with lustre as shown in image 7, but a bright orange one would look just as impressive.

For the mane, choose a bright contrasting colour, bright pink for this friend. Roll out your choice of fondant, cut out a semicircle and

Image 6.

Image 7.

Image 8.

curve it around the back of the head as shown in image 8, securing with water.

Add a cute fringe and a tail by rolling out little fat sausages and giving them a good curl as shown in images 9 and 10.

The end! The unicorn could, of course, be eating or doing all

Image 9.

sorts of things; feel free to elaborate to your heart's content. However, adding something as simple as some matching pink fringe around the cake and making the cake colour pop, she really sings just as she is.

Before you let anyone nibble on this sweet treat, don't forget to remove the cocktail sticks to prevent a nasty surprise!

Image 10.

CHAPTER NINE

Festive Friend

WHETHER YOUR HOUSEHOLD celebrates the traditional festivities at the end of the year or not, a tradition of a rich fruit cake during December is something that most of us indulge in, and what is a cake without a friend to sit on top of it? In this chapter you'll learn how to make the most festive of friends. A jolly little chap who would probably be found busily beavering away in the toy workshop. For this design we'll use polymer clay so that he can be packed away and brought out every December, but he could just as easily be made out of fondant to be gobbled up along with the cake. It is the time of year associated with over-indulgence after all.

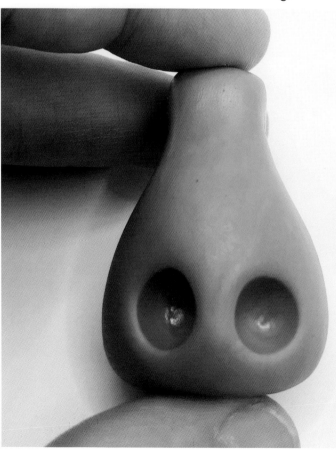

Image 2.

Remember the hygiene protocols before you begin; make sure everything is clean and you have plenty of materials for cleaning down between colour changes.

Let's start by making his body. Dust your palms with cornflour if they get too hot, to avoid the clay getting sticky, and then take a generous pinch of green clay, rolling between your palms to make a smooth ball. Start to smooth it into a triangle shape by squeezing one end into a thin top body and the other into a rounded bottom body. Smooth the corners off the fat end and push two indentations into it with the round tool as shown in image 2. It looks a bit like a nose at this stage!

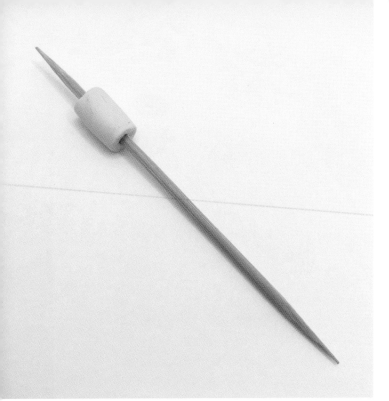

Image 3.

Image 4.

Next, push a small, thin skin-toned sausage on to a cocktail stick at one end, leaving the very end exposed as shown in image 3.

Now make the head by rolling a pinch of skin tone between your palms to make a smooth ball. Dust your palms with cornflour if they get too hot, to avoid the clay getting sticky. Roll out some white fondant and cut out two discs for the eyes, placing these on to the face and adding two tiny black balls for pupils. When placing the eyes, lay them gently on to the face and press them so that they are slightly popping out at the sides instead of smoothing them around the head. Roll a tiny ball of skin tone for the nose and add a big smiling mouth with the smiling tool as shown in image 4. Push the head on to the cocktail stick attached to the neck and then push that into the body.

For the coat let's roll out all the pieces that we'll need prior to assembly, as shown in image 5. For the main piece, roll a flat red rectangle and trim one end to be slightly narrower at the top than at the bottom, trimming with a thin sausage of white. Then roll two thin red sausages, slightly thicker at one end, and cut out a white circle and cut this in half.

Lay the body on top of the main red piece and wrap it around the top half, securing it at the neck, leaving the lower part open as shown in image 6.

Place the two semicircles around the neck to create a collar as shown in image 7.

Now on to the hair, which is very easy yet extremely effective. Roll out two orange balls, flatten them and score with a cocktail stick. Then roll out a flat oval in orange, lay it sideways and pull

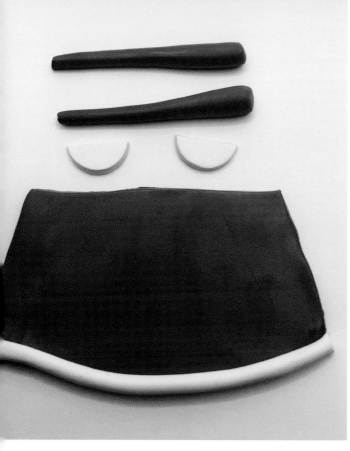

Image 5.

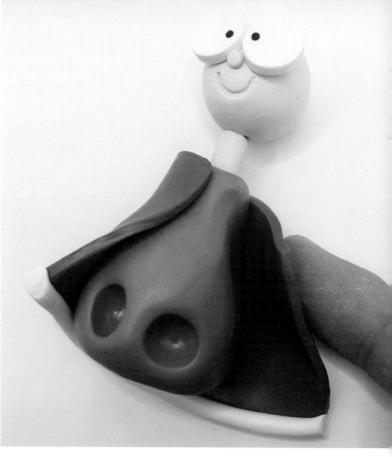

Image 6.

the bottom down into a flat edge, curling the ends slightly before scoring with a cocktail stick as shown in image 8.

Place the larger piece around the sides and back of the head and

Image 7.

Image 8.

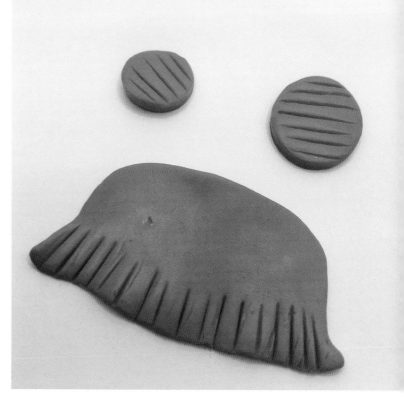

Image 9.

Image 10.

then place the two flat circles on top to create a parting as shown in image 9.

Next, add the arms, either side of the body, and add a hat by taking a ball of clay, pushing it down to flatten one end whilst pulling up on the other to create a peak. Add a thin sausage of white as a trim as shown in image 10. Then cut two tiny yellow discs and prick them twice with a cocktail stick before securing underneath the collar. Cute!

For the legs, roll out two little fat sausages in white. Each should taper at one end. Then get a very thin sausage of red and twist around each leg at a slight angle as shown in image 11.

Add little hands by rolling out two little egg shapes in skin tone and gently push them flat, dusting some cornflour on the surface and on your finger first to avoid sticking. Then take a sharp knife and cut four little slits at one end, thus creating four fingers and a thumb. If you're very careful you can separate them to create movement and wrap them around any objects your character wants to hold. Add feet by cutting out hearts and folding them in two. Add a little bell on the end of them by rolling tiny yellow balls and pricking twice with a cocktail stick as shown in image 1.

Image 11.

As with all clay creations in this book, bake this one on the lowest heat setting on your oven. Once it has reached temperature, place the topper on greaseproof paper on a baking tray and bake in the centre of the oven for twenty minutes, after which you should carefully remove from the oven and leave on a cool surface until completely cold.

Once cool, he's ready for taking his place on top of that rich fruit cake we may all indulge in.

CHAPTER TEN

And the Winner is...

THIS CHAPTER IS for the glamour lover in your life, the movie siren, the red-carpet ready award winner! This could quite easily of course be adapted to create a dashing male 'winner', but the design in this chapter is for a vintage siren complete with jewel-encrusted gown. This design is being made from fondant and because of the shapes and weight distributions each part is going to have to completely dry out before you can assemble them ready for their place on top of the cake, so if time is an issue then make this out of clay.

Image 2.

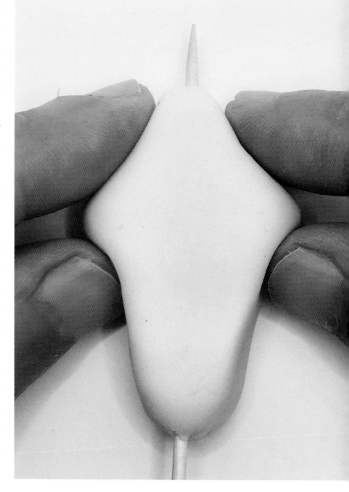

However, if you want a fun little project that takes a few days to produce, this is your new best friend and totally worth the squeals when the birthday diva is told that she can eat her mini-me if the whim should take her. A diva would probably love that.

A diva loves hygiene too, so remember the hygiene protocols before you begin; make sure everything is clean and you have plenty of materials for cleaning down between colour changes.

First up let's start making the body. Take a generous pinch of fondant that matches your character's skin tone and roll between your palms to make a smooth ball. Dust your palms with cornflour if they get too hot, to avoid the clay/fondant getting sticky. Next, push a cocktail stick through the ball, flatten the ball slightly by pushing down on your surface and then place between your hands and smooth the top into a neck and the bottom into a waist as shown in image 2.

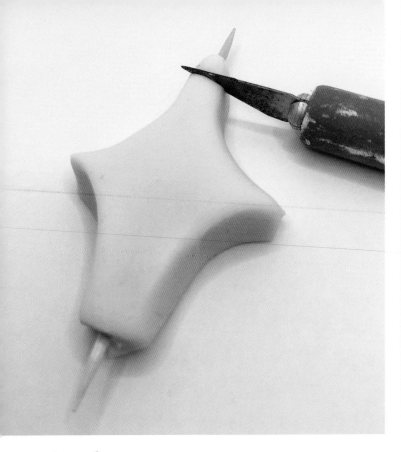

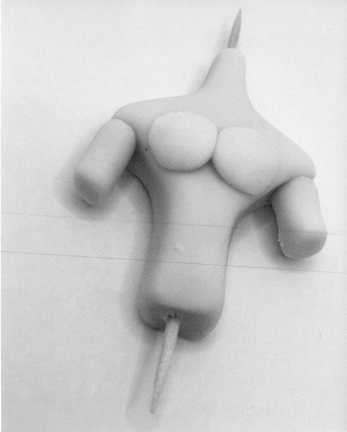

Image 3.

Image 4.

Next, smooth the sides to create the top of the shoulders and under the arms, cutting off any excess fondant, as shown in image 3.

Now roll out two small sausages to create the tops of the arms and two small balls for the boobs and secure in place with water. Flatten the boobs until smooth and give the arms nice flat ends so that the lower arm has a surface to stick to, as shown in image 4.

The face for this design is slightly different from the others in this book. Roll out a small ball for the head and secure to the neck with water. Next, cut out a small, flat purple disc and cut this in half – placing on to the face as eyelids. Roll a tiny ball for the nose. For the mouth cut out a small, flat white triangle, place this on to the face. Roll out a small, thin red line for the bottom lip and two red tear shapes for the top lip, securing everything with water as shown in image 5.

Now for the skirt! This is going to support the whole creation so don't make it too narrow or it could snap; likewise don't make it too wide or it will take forever to dry in the middle and will be heavy on top of the cake. Roll out a fat green sausage for your skirt and smooth the top of one end to create hips, and flatten the other end which is where it would hit the floor when she's standing up, as shown in image 6. Push a cocktail stick into the bottom of the topper to make a hole for a stick to go later when attaching it to the cake.

Now place everything that you've made so far in a dry but ventilated area for at least twenty-four hours so that they can

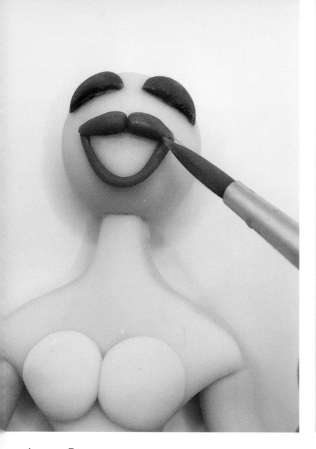

Image 5.

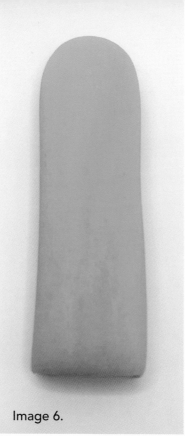

Image 6.

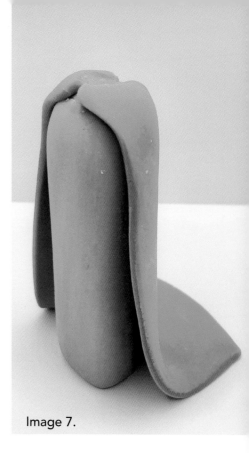

Image 7.

completely dry out. You might find it will take a bit longer than that, especially the skirt. If you can give the pieces forty-eight hours it will do it all good and no harm. Try not to cover it, you want to get the air to it to allow it to dry. Once your pieces have dried out, you can begin to assemble your diva at last! Start by rolling out a thin green rectangle. Stand the skirt up and attach the train to the top of the skirt with water as shown in image 7.

Skip this step if you don't have lustre, but if you do, the diva needs your lustre! With a thin paintbrush, add a gold edge to the train as shown in image 8 and anywhere else that you might feel that she needs it. Don't be sad if you're lustre free, she'll still look great without it. But if you do have it, feel free to give that skirt a cover too and even mix in some glitter as shown in image 1. Pure Hollywood realness, friends!

Image 8.

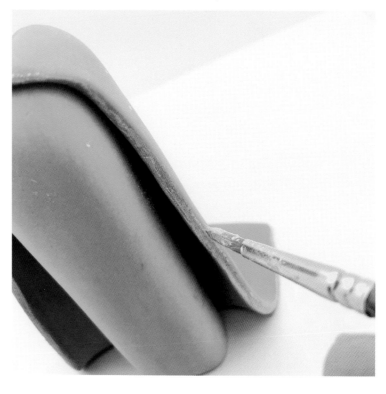

Image 9.

For the bodice, simply roll out thin, even sausages of fondant and place vertically all the way around the body as shown in image 9.

Next her hair! If you're making this as a mini version of the birthday girl then why not try creating a mini version of her hair – if her style isn't Hollywood then create fantasy hair but in her colour. It is lots of fun when people see things that mirror themselves. For this design let's start by rolling out the pieces you'll need as shown in image 10. Roll a flat oval shape to cover the back of the head, then four different pointy-ended sausages to create her curls. Keep them fat though, almost tear-shaped.

Next, lay her head on to the oval, securing the back with water as shown in image 11. Next, place two of the curls either side of her head, curling them round to join at the top as shown in image 12. Finally, add the last two curls in the same way, creating a nice curly flick at the end as shown in image 13.

Image 10.

Image 11.

Image 12.

Image 13.

Image 13.

For the lower arms, roll two small green sausages, cutting them slightly at the end so that you can bend them to create the elbows as shown in image 14. Roll a long, thin strip to place all around the body at the top of the arms. This will give a nice tidy finish to the bodice. Secure everything with water.

The award is made by stamping out a small yellow disc. Cover a small amount of a cocktail stick in fondant, leaving the bottom exposed so that it will poke into the disc. Add a star on top and secure everything with water as shown in image 15. Place the award across the body and secure with two hands. Roll out two little egg shapes in the colour of the gloves and gently push them flat, dusting some cornflour on the surface and on your finger first to avoid sticking. Then take a sharp knife and cut four little slits at one end, thus creating four fingers and a thumb! Carefully separate them to create movement and wrap them around the trophy.

Now put her back into that dry place and leave her to completely dry out for twenty-four hours. When completely dry, you can secure the top half of the body to the skirt. And you're done! All dressed up and ready to go on to the top of the cake.

Before you let anyone nibble on this sweet treat, remember to remove the cocktail sticks to prevent a nasty surprise!

Image 14.

CHAPTER ELEVEN

Little Superhero

SUPERHEROES COME IN all shapes and sizes and what better way to tell somebody that they are your hero than by making that mini warrior to perch upon their party cake? Keeping in mind the ethos that anybody can be super, the hero in this chapter isn't gendered but it is a child. Your version can, as always, be tweaked to your cake recipient's age, gender, ethnicity etc. This topper will require a checklist from the hero in question or, if it is a surprise, a list from their nearest and dearest: what is their favourite colour? Hobby? Toy? Hairstyle? Shoes? Socks? Sweets? The more personality you can give to our hero, the bigger the squeal and quite possibly the bigger the hero.

But like all good superheroes, remember the hygiene protocols before you begin; make sure everything is clean and you have plenty of materials for cleaning down between colour changes.

This design is being made from fondant, and because of the weight distributions each part is going to have to completely dry

Image 2.

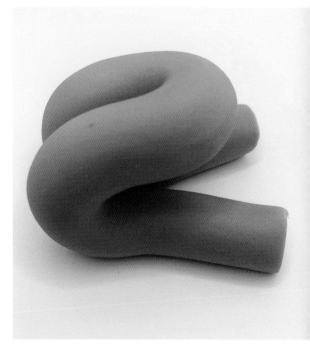

out before you can assemble them ready for their place on top of the cake, so if time is an issue then make this out of clay. However, if you want a project that you can keep going back to for a few days then proceed with fondant and glee! The glee will no doubt be shared by the excited birthday hero when they find out that they can eat themselves.

Let's start with the legs. Take a generous pinch of fondant that matches your character's skin tone and roll between your palms to make a smooth sausage. Dust your palms with cornflour if they get too hot, to avoid the fondant getting sticky. Take the sausage and fold it in half, and then again to create the kneeling position as shown in image 2.

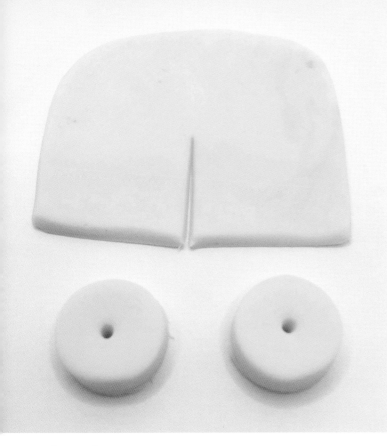

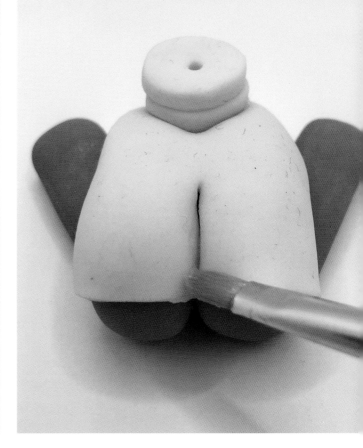

Image 3.

Image 4.

Image 5.

To make the shorts, roll out a thin yellow oval and cut it in half, discarding one half. Make a small cut with a knife halfway through the surviving piece to create the legs of the shorts. Then cut out two small yellow discs, cutting holes through the middle of them with a cocktail stick as shown in image 3.

Place the shorts on top of the legs and smooth down the sides and the back, covering the exposed skin. Place the two discs on top, securing everything with water as shown in image 4.

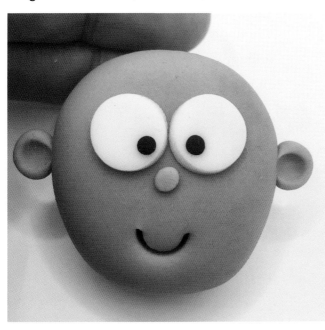

Next it is time for the head. Take a pinch of fondant that matches your character's skin tone and roll between your palms to make a smooth ball. Again, dust your palms with cornflour if they get too hot, to avoid the fondant getting sticky. Roll out some white fondant and cut out two discs for the eyes, placing these on to the face and adding two tiny black balls for pupils. Roll a tiny ball of skin tone for the nose and add a big smiley mouth with the smiling tool, securing everything with water as shown in image 5.

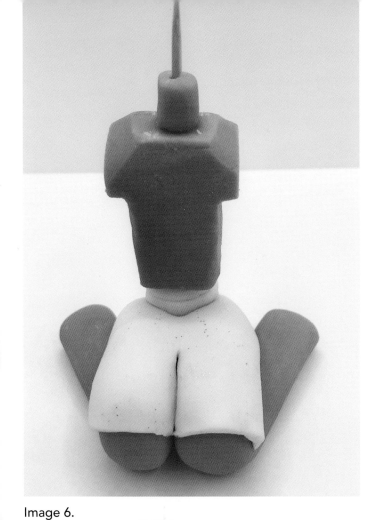

Image 6.

Image 7.

Image 8.

Create the body by shaping a rectangle in skin tone and cutting in a little narrower underneath each arm – think T-shirt shape. Add a small sausage for the neck and push a cocktail stick through both the neck and body through the two small discs attached to the top of the legs as shown in image 6.

The vest is very easy – roll out a long blue rectangle and cut a small hole in the middle of it as shown in image 7.

Lift the rectangle over the neck and secure either side with water to the body, leaving the arm holes exposed as shown in image 8.

Now it is time to make the superhero's favourite things; this

Image 9.

hero loves their favourite toys – the frog and the dog. Take a look at image 9. It really is all fairly straightforward, a body, two arms and legs for each and both have oval heads. Create the striped, furry look for the dog by reading Chapter 5 of this book 'The Furry Family Member'.

For the arms, roll two thin sausages in skin tone and bend to create elbows. For the slingshot, roll two short fat sausages in brown,

Image 10.

bend one to a right angle and place it on top of the other to create the Y-shape. Next, roll a thin piece of black to create the elastic and finish with a little flat disc. I've finished mine off by drawing some wood marks on with edible ink as shown in image 10.

Image 11.

Now it is time to assemble. Take the slingshot and place it on one side of the figure, place the arm on top – securing with water. On the other side add the head and the body of the dog as shown in image 11.

Image 12.

Next, add the dog's paws poking over the figure's arms. On the other side, add the frog's head and arms on top of the right arm, as if the arm is squeezing them and they are poking out over it. Add the hands and secure everything with water as shown in image 12. Hands are much easier to create than you might first think. Roll out

Image 13.

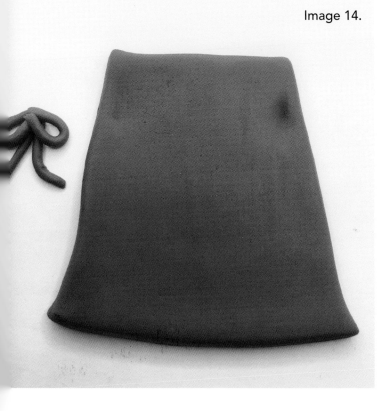

Image 14.

two little egg shapes in skin tone and gently push them flat, dusting some cornflour on the surface and on your finger first to avoid sticking. Then take a sharp knife and cut four little slits at one end, thus creating four fingers and a thumb! If you're very careful you can separate them to create movement and wrap them around objects your character wants to hold, in this case the superhero's favourite toys.

Back to the head, it is time for some superhero realness hair. This figure has afro hair which we will create by rolling lots of different-sized black balls and covering the head with them. Really easy, really therapeutic and really effective. For the mask, roll out a thin red rectangle. Cut out two eye holes and pinch the right and left ends to make them smaller. Cut tiny diamonds where the nose would go and in between the eyes and lay the mask over the eyeholes, securing everything with water as shown in image 13.

To make the cape, roll out a thin rectangle, pulling it out slightly at the bottom to make it wider. Roll out thin sausages of red to create the bow for the neck as shown in image 14.

Image 15.

Drape the cape from the shoulders all the way down the back, adding the bow to the front and securing everything with water as shown in image 15.

Make the socks by rolling out two stubby white sausages. Flatten one end and roll the other between your fingers, making it smaller and more pointed. Add lines with a knife to create rolls in the sides of the sock as shown in image 16.

Last but not least, this superhero needs

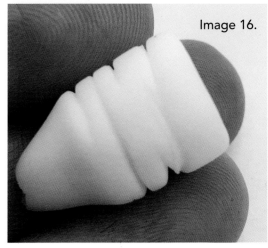

Image 16.

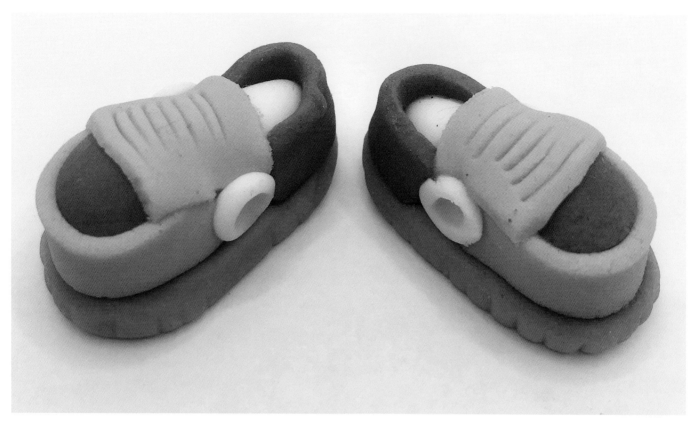

Image 17.

sneakers. We went into great detail on how to make the perfect brightly coloured sneaker in Chapter 6 of this book, 'The Gamer'. Pop on over and have a look for detailed instructions and step-by-step images on how to make the perfect sneaker. This design has equally bright colours – pink, blue and orange with yellow buttons as shown in image 17.

Attach the sock to the end of the ankle and the sneaker to the end of the sock, securing everything with water. Lastly, add the legs to the frog and the dog as shown in image 1.

Now I think you'll find it is time for this superhero to meet their bigger-me and for the pair to go and save the day. It is cake time!!

A quick reminder: before you let anyone nibble on this sweet treat, remember to remove the cocktail sticks to prevent a nasty surprise!

CHAPTER TWELVE

Wedding Day

THIS IS THE big one. Responsibility-wise, if somebody is asking you to make a cake topper for them, the one that sits on top of their wedding cake is the one that you really want to get right. Not that you don't want them all to be perfect but a wonky arm on a unicorn is charming, a wonky arm on the bride is awkward. So you'll be happy to hear that not only is this the perfect show stopper, but it is also very easy to make. 'Not as easy as the pig,' I hear you cry! True, but the only difference between the two is time. This is still playing, just for longer. So enjoy it! This topper is being made from polymer clay so that the lucky lovers get to keep it after the cake has been eaten, but if you prefer you can use fondant. The only difference is that, once made, a fondant design will need a good week to dry out versus clay taking twenty minutes to bake, so it is whatever works best for you and your schedule.

Don't forget the hygiene protocols before you begin; make sure everything is clean and you have plenty of materials to hand for cleaning down between colour changes.

To begin with, roll out a large piece of clay approximately 2cm thick and cut out a long rectangle. Next, curve off the top two corners, thus creating an arch. Your characters will sit inside this arch so make it as big or as small as is required for your cake. Next, cut out lots of little flat discs and tiny balls and then unleash your creativity, placing them wherever you feel looks best – see image 2. Although not intentional, initially, this gives a background that's almost stained glass in its effect.

Next, roll out two long, thin sausages to create the surrounding of

Image 2.

Image 3.

Image 4.

the arch. In this design we're going for a gold arch using lustre (see Chapter 1), but do feel free to choose your own colour scheme, the gold is very much optional. Take your thin sausages and after pinching two of the ends together twist them around each other to create one long twist. If you have gold lustre this will work best painted on black clay, it really makes it pop – see image 3.

Next, place the twist around the arch and gently push against the base to bind them together. Don't press too hard, the majority of the fusing together will take place during the baking process and you don't want to dent your twist – see image 4. Gently push a cocktail stick into the each of the two ends of the twist. Only push in 3cm of the stick, leaving the remainder of the cocktail stick visible so that it can be pushed into the finished cake, thus allowing your completed design to stand securely. It is important to do this now and not at the end as your design will be much more fragile once the characters have been made and secured.

Now it is time to cut out the wedding outfits! Don't be overwhelmed by the number of pieces you're being asked to cut out in image 5. There are a lot, but you'll find it much easier to prepare them all first and then assemble.

Start with the body by rolling out a fat pink sausage, rounded at the top and flattened at the bottom. Next, make the legs from one long blue sausage. Only one arm is visible so one blue sausage for the arm, two skin-toned balls for the head and neck, and a rectangle of blue for the jacket. The collars for the shirt are two tiny pink triangles, make the same for the bow tie in blue. The waistcoat is

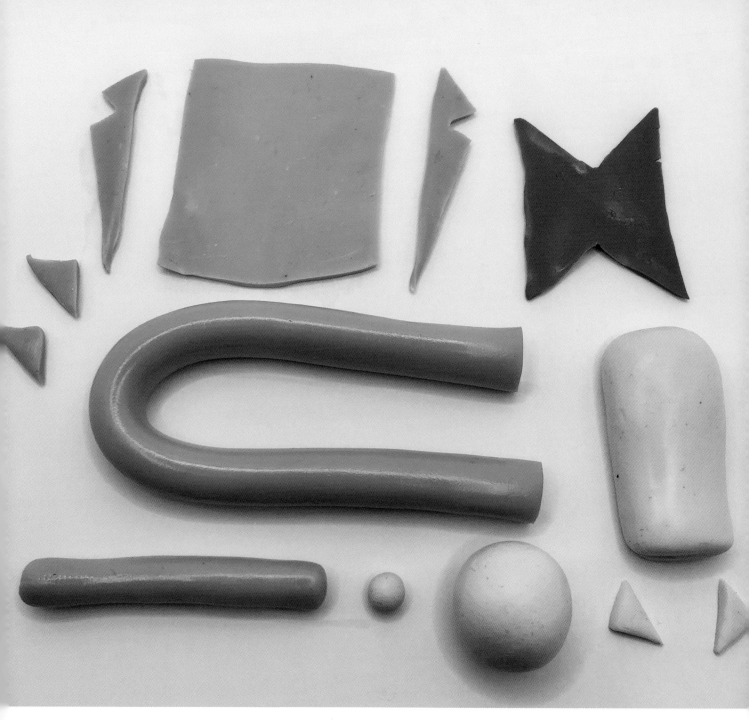

made from a contrasting blue rectangle with triangles cut out at the top and bottom.

Finally, (phew!) the lapels for the jacket – which look a bit fiddly but they are just two thin rectangles the length of the jacket with angles cut out of them. See? Nothing to be overwhelmed about! Honestly, now that's done I can tell you that that was the fiddliest bit. Well done. You can do anything now!

The bride is by comparison incredibly easy. The body is made in a similar way to the body in Chapter 10, 'And the Winner is…', but this time we're not covering the body in clothes, this is the

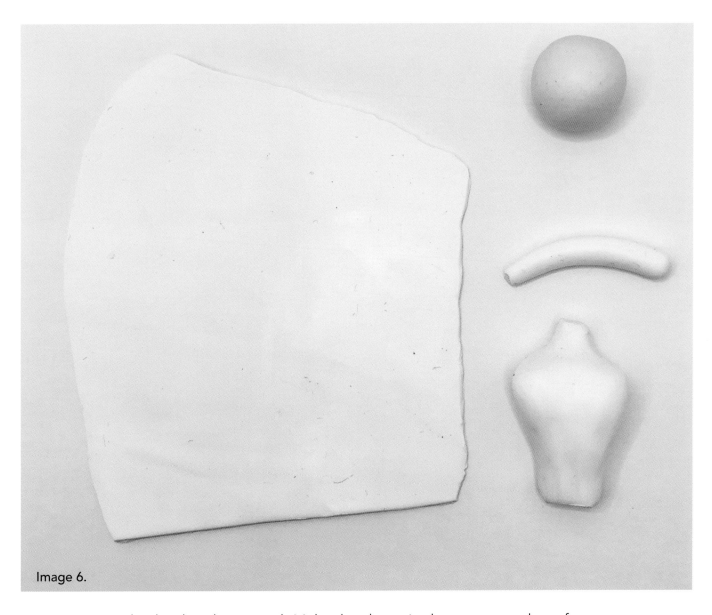

Image 6.

body, already covered. Make the shape in the same way, but after adding the boobs smooth the clay down to create the torso, bust, shoulders and neck in one piece as shown in image 6.

Next, roll out one thin white sausage for her arm, a smooth, round skin-tone ball for the head and a large rectangle of white for the skirt, keeping it wider at one end. Don't roll the skirt too thinly as you want the shape to be able to hold itself – too thin and it will probably sink in on itself whilst baking and seeing as she has no legs under that skirt, it probably wouldn't be a good look!

Now it is time to start to bring all of the pieces you've made together. Firstly, let's put the male figure in place as shown in image 7.

Image 7.

Image 8.

Image 9.

Start by folding the long sausage in half to create the legs and place them at the bottom of the arch, leaving a little room for his feet to go on later. Next, lay the jacket piece above the trousers and then on top of that place the pink body. Score a cocktail stick along the front of the pink shirt and prick a line of dots to replicate buttons and then place the waistcoat on top of that, folding it round to cover most of the pink body. Then fold either side of the jacket back around the waistcoat, leaving the jacket open slightly. Place the neck on top of the pink body and the head on top of the neck, pressing very gently to secure them in place.

Next, add the collar to the shirt, the lapels to the jacket and then the bow tie as shown in image 8.

Now it is time to put the bride in place. Your best bet is to start with the head – is she taller or shorter than her groom? Once you've placed her head where you're happy with it, gently press it down to secure it and then place her body underneath it, pressing down gently to secure this too as shown in image 9.

This is the exciting bit where it all starts to come to life: the flowing bridal skirt! This is also where you'll find that clay will do things that fondant would struggle with. Start by gathering the top of the skirt so that it is waist size, pinching it together and then tucking it in on

Image 10.

itself to reveal the gathered, pleated waist. Carefully push this into place underneath the torso. Next, pull the bottom of the skirt out, opening up the pleats so that it sweeps to the left, covering the bottom of the arch. Add both of their arms, bending at the elbows and reaching towards each other as shown in image 10.

Now it is time to create your faces. How you want to do this is completely up to you; there might be very specific features of your couple that you want to capture and by all means do feel free to adapt to your own requirements. We've kept it simple and cartoon-like with this design. Using the tool with the ball on the end of it,

Image 11.

gently push indentations where you want the eyes to be. Roll a tiny ball of skin tone for each of their noses and add big smiling mouths with the smiling tool as shown in image 11.

Now for the hair – so easy considering the grandeur of the occasion! First roll out two thin sausages to go from one side of the bride's head to the other and tuck them gently underneath either side of her neck. For the groom, roll one thin sausage to go around his head as you have done with the bride but instead of placing a second one on top, roll two small, thin sausages, one for either side of his head and then three more that grow ever so slightly longer than the other, placed on top of his head to create a fringe, flicking the ends up as shown in image 12. Add tiny black balls to the eyes for pupils and don't forget to have the lovebirds looking at each other.

Image 12.

Image 12.

Now add eyebrows to both characters by rolling tiny thin sausages; place them at a jaunty angle to make the characters look instantly smitten. Finally, it is time to give the bride her crowning glory! Roll out five long, thin sausages in the bride's hair colour, thinning the ends out to a fine point to allow them to flick at both ends. Give her a side parting and curl two of the sausages on the right-hand side and three on the left-hand side, layering them on top of each other and mirroring the wave of each other as shown in image 13.

Again, this is something that would be ridiculously fragile in fondant, but in clay you can get away with much more delicate hairstyles. Take a little white ball and squash it slightly between your fingers to create the perfect pillbox hat and place it across her parting at an angle. Gorgeous, right?

Cut out tiny flowers and leaves to decorate the arch with as shown in image 1, all the better if they match the cake or the wedding colours. For the hands, roll out little egg shapes in skin tone and gently push them flat, dusting some cornflour on the surface and on your finger first to avoid sticking. Place them over each other so that the couple are holding hands. Lastly, add two brown sausages for the groom's feet and the creation is ready for the oven. This is daunting, I know, but it will be fine. As with all clay creations in this book, bake this one on the lowest heat setting on your oven. Once it has reached temperature, place the topper on greaseproof paper on a baking tray and bake in the centre of the oven for twenty-five minutes, after which you should carefully remove from the oven and leave on a cool surface until completely cold.

All that's left to do is to wish the happy couple the very best for their cake-filled future and to place them proudly on top of that top tier.

CHAPTER THIRTEEN

Cheeky Princess

IT WAS OBVIOUSLY important to include a princess topper in this book because despite wanting to avoid obvious choices, the fact is that a LOT of little people want to be princesses on their birthdays and a princess cake is a regular request. In this chapter you'll learn how to put a twist on the classic princess figure and this will require a very important checklist from the little person in question: what is your favourite colour? Toy? Hairstyle? Shoes? Socks? Sweets? The more details you can add to personalise the design, the bigger the squeal. So dig deep! Hopefully, it goes without saying that both boys and girls will squeal at this cake, there is absolutely no limit on who can be a princess! This design is being made from fondant and because of the shapes and weight distributions each part is going to have to completely dry out before you can assemble them ready for their place on top of the cake, so if time is an issue then make this out of clay. However, if you want a fun little project that takes a few days to produce, this is a great little one and definitely worth the squeals when the birthday princess is told that they can eat their mini-me, should the whim take them. Yummy!

As always, remember the hygiene protocols before you begin; make sure everything is clean and you have plenty of materials for cleaning down between colour changes.

Let's start with the face by taking a generous pinch of fondant that matches your character's skin tone and roll between your palms to make a smooth ball. Dust your palms with cornflour if they get too hot, to avoid the fondant getting sticky. Instead of having a round head we want this character to have a real toy-like quality to it so when you have your round head, place it on a floured surface and flatten it ever so slightly on both sides to create a fat disc. Next, roll

Image 2.

out some white fondant and cut out two discs for the eyes, placing these on to the face and adding two tiny black balls for pupils. Roll two tiny balls of pink for the cheeks and add a mouth with the smiling tool, securing them with water as shown in image 2.

Next, roll out some yellow fondant and cut out a circle the same shape as the head and place the head on top of it, securing with water.

Then roll out three thin yellow sausages and wrap them from one side of her head to the other. Next, roll two little red balls to create the hairbands and place them either side of her head. Push a cocktail stick right through the middle of the head through both of the red balls as shown in image 3. Keep the cocktail stick exposed at each end – that's where you'll attach the pigtails later. Finally, score a knife through the centre of the yellow sausages to create a centre parting.

Now it is time to make the body, which is made in the same way as the diva in Chapter 11. Take a generous pinch of fondant in skin

Image 3.

Image 4.

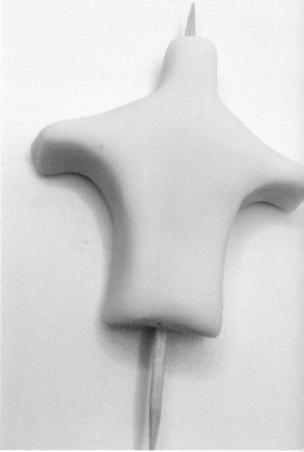

tone and roll between your palms to make a smooth ball. Dust your palms with cornflour if they get too hot, to avoid the fondant getting sticky. Next, push a cocktail stick through the ball, flatten the ball slightly by pushing down on your surface and then place between your hands and smooth the top into a neck and the bottom into a waist. Next, smooth the sides to create the top of the shoulders and under the arms, cutting off any excess fondant as shown in image 4.

Now place everything that you've made so far in a dry but ventilated area for at least twenty-four hours so that they can completely dry out. You might find it will take a bit longer than that. If you can give the pieces forty-eight hours it will do it all good and no harm. Try not to cover it, you want to get the air to it to allow it to dry.

The T-shirt is very simple – roll out a long pink rectangle and cut a small hole in the middle of it as shown in image 5. Next, cut out small rectangles in all four corners.

Now lift the shape over the neck and secure either side with water to the body, leaving the arm holes exposed as shown in image 6.

Image 5.

Image 6.

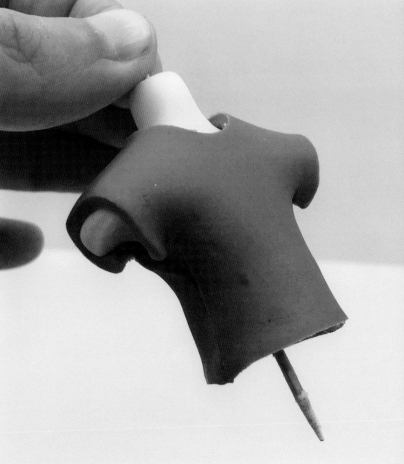

Image 7.

Image 8.

To make the legs, roll out two thin sausages in skin tone and wrap the ends in a contrasting colour to create the socks as shown in image 7.

Next on to the skirt. Roll out a circle and cover it with a design that goes all the way around. If you don't have cutters to create a design as shown in image 8, rolling little balls in different colours and shapes will be just as effective, maybe even more so.

Then take a small ball of fondant, colour unimportant as it won't be seen, and push the legs into it to create a seated position on the floor with the legs apart. Next, take your skirt and place it on top so that the feet are poking out as shown in image 9.

Image 9.

Now it is time to fill the birthday girl's arms with her favourite things. This princess is going to be clutching her favourite toy and an enormous lollipop. Pop over to Chapter 11 and the little superhero for a how-to on making toys. Lollipops are very simple – just roll a

Image 10.

long, thin sausage of fondant in on itself like a snail shape, push a cocktail stick through and decorate accordingly. Start by placing all of the separate parts of the toy – except the arms – on to the body, securing with water as shown in image 10.

Next, roll two thin skin-toned sausages for the arms. Add the lollipop and then the arms, securing the ends under the T-shirt

Image 11.

sleeves with water. Then add the arms of the toy on top of the princess's arms so that they appear to be poking out from her embrace. Lastly, add hands by rolling two little egg shapes and gently push them flat, dusting some cornflour on the surface and on your finger first to avoid sticking. Then take a sharp knife and cut four little slits at one end, thus creating four fingers and a thumb. See image 11.

To make the shoes, start by cutting out all of the green pieces in image 12. Cut a thin, flat circle in half, roll two thin sausages and two thin, flat rectangles.

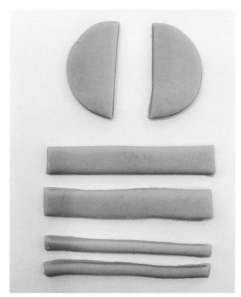

Image 12.

Next, the soles of the shoes. If you roll out two little fat brown sausages, you should be able to flatten them easily enough to create the rounded sole shape. Score across them all with a knife to create the grips on the bottom of a shoe as shown in image 13. Next, roll out two little fat sausages for the feet; make them the same colour as the socks. Place them on top of the soles, wrapping the thin green rectangle around the back and covering the two with the semicircle – securing everything with water as shown in image 14. Next, take the thin sausage and place it across the join as shown in image 15. Then add a little embellishment to the side where a fastening would be, as shown in image 16.

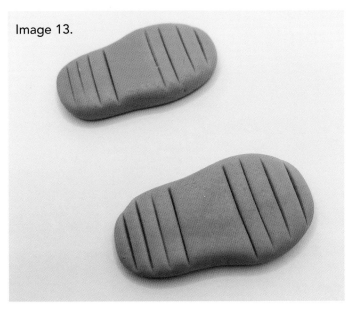

Image 13.

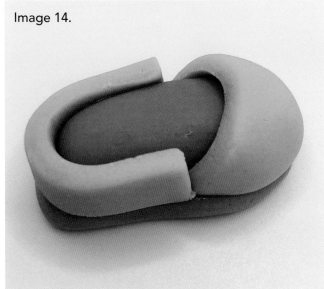

Image 14.

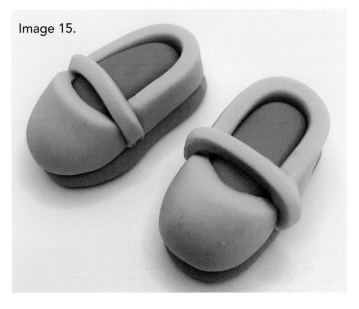

Image 15.

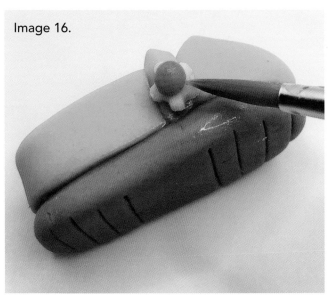

Image 16.

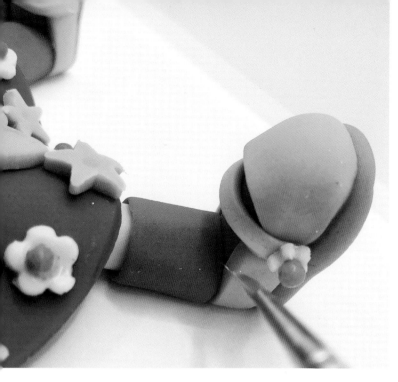

Image 17.

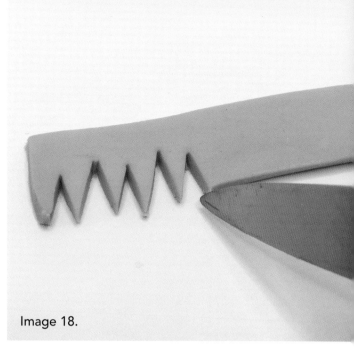

Image 18.

And that's the shoes made! Cute, eh? Secure them to the legs with water as shown in image 17.

Now the birthday princess needs her crown. Roll out a long, thin rectangle and cut little triangles out of it as shown in image 18.

With a little water, join the ends together as shown in image 19.

Finally, add a thin sausage to pipe the bottom of the crown, and let it dry so that she can wear it at a jaunty angle. All that's left to do is to pop her head on top of her neck, add two tear shapes for bunches and sit that crown on her head – see image 1. Time for her to meet her bigger-me!

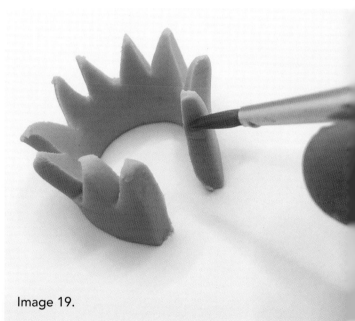

Image 19.

Before you let anyone nibble on this sweet treat, remember to remove the cocktail sticks to prevent a nasty surprise!

Where to next...?

THAT BRINGS US to the end of our journey together, friends. Thank you for choosing both this book and this creative journey; I hope the toppers were as fun and rewarding for you to make as they were for me to create and that you are leaving this book not only armed with new skills and knowledge but also that you are inspired. Whilst it is the end of the book, I hope it is just the beginning of something wonderful for you.

My beginning happened many years ago when I was visiting a friend and her children. We were having a crafting afternoon and in between judging macaroni landscapes and participating in a fashion doll beauty contest (I won), I was absentmindedly playing with some children's clay. 'What is that?' my friend asked me. I produced a tiny bowl of fruit, perched proudly in my palm. 'How did you do that?' she squealed. 'Anybody can do that!' I laughed. 'No, they can't!' she said. In that moment I realised that I'd got quite a thrill from bringing somebody joy by creating something out of nothing. I quickly made a tiny version of my friend and she squealed. I made a tiny version of her cat, she squealed. 'You should make cake toppers' she said.

And so, I did. I bought myself some fondant and clay and spent a couple of evenings each week playing, making friends with the materials and seeing what worked and what didn't. It's fair to say that some of my earlier attempts weren't perfect, but I was still pleased as punch with them and I was having lots of fun. I improved with practice and I'm not ashamed to say I'm possibly a bit addicted to finding a cake to top and now there is nothing that I wouldn't be confident attempting.

As well as a maker, I'm also a keen baker and I have made lots of cakes for lots of people, all of them covered in my creations. As well as the joy and the squeals, the thing I'm always asked is: 'how did you do that?' and I have always said the same thing: 'anybody can do it'. I truly believe that anybody can make things if they're shown how and it has been a treat to share my knowledge. It is SO satisfying to create stuff. In a world where we have become all too used to putting the things we need straight into an online shopping basket, making the choice and taking the time to create things with your own fair hands should be encouraged and enjoyed. 'Who made that?' they'll ask. 'I did!' you can proudly reply!

It is now time for you to explore your own imagination and creativity; the possibilities of where you go next are endless because without realising it you have become a maker and you can make anything if you put your mind to it. A pirate ship full of scoundrels? A play pen full of toddlers? A dancefloor full of divas? Have a look below at some of my crazy creations to whet your appetite and go ahead and ride your own creative rainbow. If you post any of your fabulous creations online, please add the hashtag #makeyourowncaketoppers so that we can #squeal for you. This book also has its own Instagram page at @makeyourowncaketoppers, so feel free to reach out with any questions and give us a follow to see what's coming next.